MAR – 8 2016

3 1994 01545 6202

SANTA ANA PUBLIC LIBRARY

D0759234

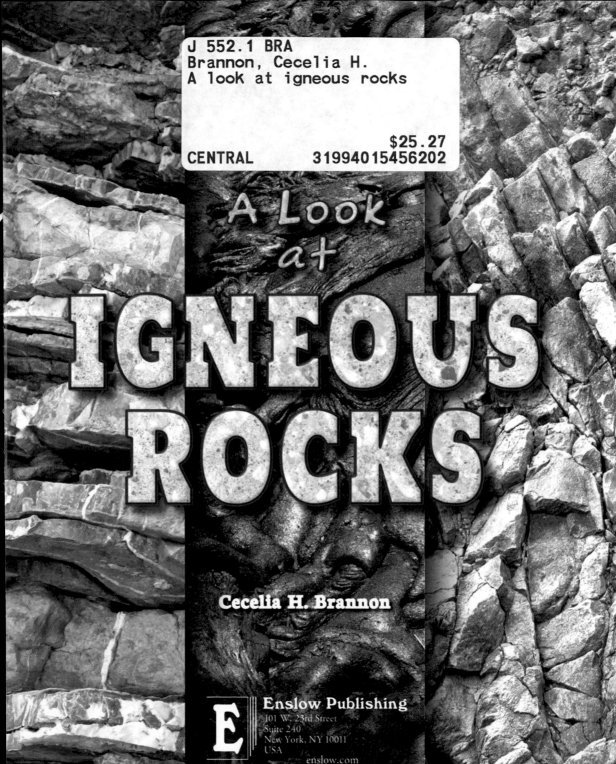

J 552.1 BRA
Brannon, Cecelia H.
A look at igneous rocks

$25.27
CENTRAL   31994015456202

A Look at IGNEOUS ROCKS

Cecelia H. Brannon

Enslow Publishing
101 W. 23rd Street
Suite 240
New York, NY 10011
USA

enslow.com

Published in 2016 by Enslow Publishing, LLC
101 W. 23rd Street, Suite 240, New York, NY 10011

Copyright © 2016 by Enslow Publishing, LLC

All rights reserved.

No part of this book may be reproduced by any means without the written permission of the publisher.

Library of Congress Cataloging-in-Publication Data

Brannon, Cecelia H., author.
  A look at igneous rocks / Cecelia H. Brannon.
      pages cm. — (The rock cycle)
  Audience: Ages 8+
  Audience: Grades 4 to 6.
  Includes bibliographical references and index.
  ISBN 978-0-7660-7318-0 (library binding)
  ISBN 978-0-7660-7316-6 (pbk.)
  ISBN 978-0-7660-7317-3 (6-pack)
  1. Igneous rocks—Juvenile literature. 2. Geochemical cycles—Juvenile literature. I. Title.
  QE461.B73 2016
  552.1—dc23
                          2015029178
Printed in the United States of America

To Our Readers: We have done our best to make sure all websites in this book were active and appropriate when we went to press. However, the author and the publisher have no control over and assume no liability for the material available on those websites or any websites they may link to. Any comments or suggestions can be sent by e-mail to customerservice@enslow.com.

Photo Credits: Cover, p. 1 a_v_d/Shutterstock.com (right), www.sandatlas.org/Shutterstock.com (lava, center), katatonia82/Shutterstock.com (left), Sakarin Sawasdinaka/Shutterstock.com (background textures throughout book), M. Niebuhr/Shutterstock.com (basaltic igneous rock, back right), kaband/Shutterstock.com (back left), vagabond54/Shutterstock.com (columnar basalt, tagline); Christine Yarusi (series logo, four-rock dingbat); p. 4 Vadim Petrakov/Shutterstock.com; p. 6 beboy/Shutterstock.com; p. 7 ZeWrestler/Wikimedia Commons/Rockcycle2.jpg/public domain; p. 9 Webspark/Shutterstock.com; p. 11 Rainer Lesniewski/Shutterstock.com (top), Vadim Petrakov/Shutterstock.com (bottom); p. 12 De Agostini Picture Library/Getty Images; p. 13 bragin Alexey/Shutterstock.com; p. 14 Freddy Thuerig/Shutterstock.com; pp. 15, 25 (bottom) ChinellatoPhoto/Shutterstock.com; p. 16 Olga_Pheonix/Shutterstock.com; p. 18 Radoslaw Lecyk/Shutterstock.com, p. 19 Ulet Ifansasti/Getty Images News/Getty Images; p. 20 Only Fabrizio/Shutterstock.com; p. 21 Vladislav S/Shutterstock.com (top), Pierre Leclerc/Shutterstock.com (bottom); p. 22 anshar/Shutterstock.com; p. 23 © iStockphoto.com/Devasahayam Chandra Dhas; p. 24 Nicholas Peter Gavin Davies/Shutterstock.com; p. 25 Patrick Poendi/Shutterstock.com (top); p. 27 WitR/Shutterstock.com (top); Aleksandar Todorovic/Shutterstock.com (bottom); p. 28 Bryan Busovicki/Shutterstock.com; p. 29 Richard A McMillin/Shutterstock.com.

Contents

What Are Igneous Rocks? 5

How Are Igneous Rocks Formed? 10

Different Types of Igneous Rocks 17

Why Are Igneous Rocks Important? 26

Glossary 30

Further Reading 31

Index 32

Lava from a volcano cooled and hardened into igneous rock.

What Are IGNEOUS ROCKS?

When you look outside, you see that rocks are everywhere. Earth's surface is made out of rock. All rocks are made of matter called **minerals** and belong to one of three different groups: **igneous**, **sedimentary**, and **metamorphic**.

Made From Magma

Igneous rocks are formed when hot magma, or liquid rock, from a volcanic eruption solidifies. The magma can become trapped in pockets of air beneath layers of the Earth's crust, where they slowly cool and harden into igneous rocks.

This eruption in Hawaii will create igneous rocks on Earth's crust.

What Are **IGNEOUS ROCKS?**

When a volcano erupts, magma is forced to the surface where it cools and hardens very quickly, which creates a different kind of igneous rock. The formation of these rocks is key to the rock cycle.

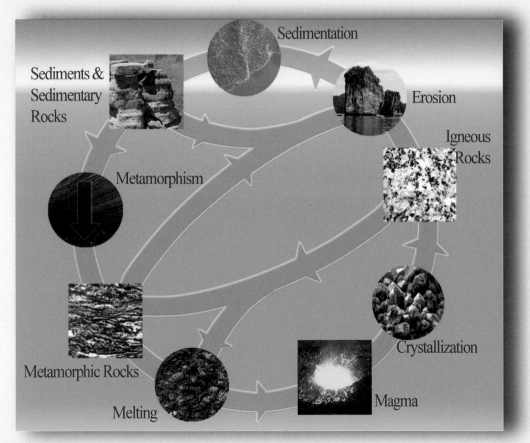

This diagram shows how old rocks break down and form new rocks through the rock cycle. Magma cools and hardens into igneous rock.

A Look at IGNEOUS ROCKS

The rock cycle starts when hot magma rises to the surface of Earth. Once there, the magma cools and hardens into igneous rocks. Over time, these igneous rocks are worn down by wind and water. In the end, they become sedimentary rocks, which can be pushed under the crust through movements such as earthquakes.

The sedimentary rocks under the surface, as well as the igneous rocks that have formed underground, are changed into metamorphic rocks through heat and pressure. Magma melts these metamorphic rocks and is then pushed to the surface or becomes trapped within Earth. When magma cools, it forms new igneous rocks below and above ground. Then the rock cycle begins again.

What Are **IGNEOUS ROCKS?**

Did You Know?

Earth is made up of layers. The crust is the top layer and made of rock. The layer of magma beneath the crust is the mantle. Below the mantle is Earth's core, which is divided into two layers. The outer core is made up of melted metals, while the inner core is a ball of solid metal.

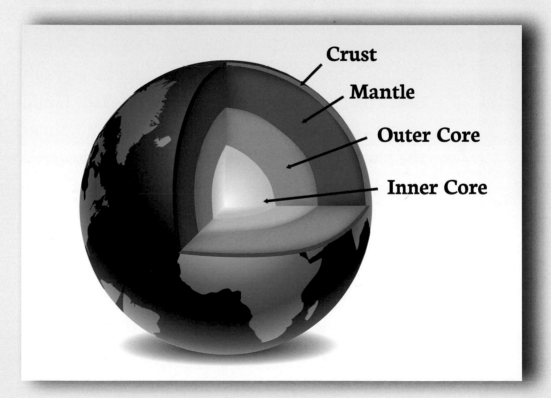

Crust

Mantle

Outer Core

Inner Core

How Are IGNEOUS ROCKS FORMED?

Earth's crust is broken into enormous sections called **plates**. These plates float on top of the liquid magma that makes up Earth's mantle. Sometimes the plates rub against each other, which creates a fault line. Fault lines are weak places in Earth's crust. Volcanoes form when magma flows into these fault lines.

Heat and pressure inside Earth force the magma up through the fault line and out onto Earth's surface. Magma cools into rock and over time can build up to form a volcanic mountain. As the volcano continues to erupt and send out lava, the lava hardens to form igneous rocks.

How Are **IGNEOUS ROCKS FORMED?**

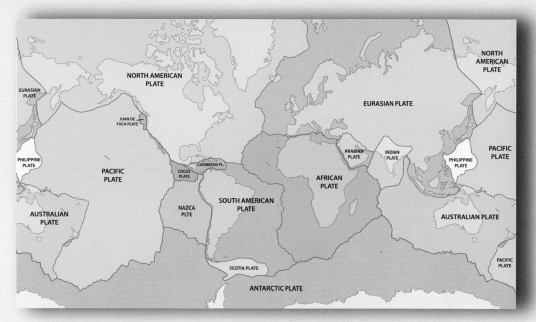

The tectonic plates that make up Earth's crust are an important part of the rock cycle.

Did You Know?

The term *igneous* comes from the Latin word *ignis*, which means "fire." This fiery rock is still liquid at its center.

This diagram shows the path magma travels during a volcanic eruption. Once forced out of Earth's surface, it flows down the slopes of the volcano.

The Cooling Process

Intrusive igneous rocks form when a pool of magma becomes trapped in a small pocket under Earth's crust. It cools slowly, and after thousands of years, it hardens into igneous rock.

When magma cools slowly, the minerals that are inside the rock form large crystals. If you look at an igneous rock called granite, you can often see colorful spots. These are the crystals of different minerals inside the rock.

Sometimes magma is forced to the surface of Earth's crust. Here, it cools quickly. These magma rocks cool too fast to form large crystals. Some cool so quickly they have no time to create crystals at all. These are called **extrusive** rocks.

Granite is an intrusive igneous rock. You can see the large crystals in it with the naked eye.

When lava cools quickly it creates a type of igneous rock called extrusive rock.

Rocks From Space

Some igneous rocks form in outer space far away from Earth. Mercury, Venus, and Mars are made of igneous rocks, just as most of Earth is. Sometimes pieces of these planets break off and join **asteroids** in their travels through space. These pieces are called **meteorites**. Meteorites sometimes hit planets while traveling through space. Each year about nineteen thousand meteorites land on Earth. Most are small, but some are large enough to damage houses or cars.

This may look like any other igneous rock on Earth, but it's not. Meteorites from Mars are made of an igneous rock called pyroxenite.

Did You Know?

Even our moon is made of igneous rocks! Some of the rocks that make up the moon appear white. These rocks are called anorthosite, norite, and troctolite. The dark parts of the moon are basalt. This happened when meteorites and other space matter hit the moon so hard that they broke the surface. Lava oozed out of these breaks in the moon's crust. When the lava cooled, it created basalt.

Different Types of IGNEOUS ROCKS

There are two groups of igneous rocks: volcanic and plutonic. Volcanic, or extrusive, rocks are formed when lava cools after a volcanic eruption. Because the lava cools quickly, these rocks have small crystals. The hardened lava forms igneous rock around the volcano, which makes it taller.

There are two types of lava. Basaltic lava flows quickly and smoothly, so it forms volcanoes with sloping sides. Rhyolitic lava is thicker and slower, which creates volcanoes with steep sides. Rhyolitic eruptions are strong enough to toss lava and rock miles (kilometers) away from the volcano.

Lava flows in Hawaii and will cool to form extrusive rocks.

Did You Know?

Mount Sinabung in Indonesia began erupting in June 2015. Thousands of residents were evacuated from their homes when the volcano began shooting smoke and ash 2,300 feet (700 meters) in the air.

Kinds of Extrusive Rocks

There are many kinds of extrusive rocks. Obsidian can form when basaltic or rhyolitic lava pours into a body of water. When lava comes in contact with water, it cools too quickly for crystals to form, which leaves a smooth and shiny rock with a glasslike texture.

Obsidian, also called volcanic glass, is usually black, but it can also be dark green or reddish brown.

Pumice is another kind of extrusive rock. It forms from rhyolitic eruptions. When this rock is formed, the lava cools so quickly that the air has no time to escape and the rock forms tiny air-filled holes. These holes make pumice the lightest rock on Earth. It can even float in water.

Different Types of IGNEOUS ROCKS

Pumice has many uses. It can be washed with denim to give jeans a soft, faded appearance. It is also used to help remove dead cells from rough skin, such as from the bottom of your feet.

Basalt rocks form from basaltic eruptions. Basalt rocks are usually black and rough. They cover ocean floors because of underwater volcanic eruptions. Basalt can be thousands of feet (meters) thick and can stretch over many miles (kilometers). Sometimes after basalt cools, it breaks and forms six-sided columns.

The Giant's Causeway in Northern Ireland is made of basalt columns. Some of these columns are more than 20 feet (6 m) high!

Kinds of Intrusive Rock

The second type of igneous rock is called plutonic, or more commonly, intrusive. Intrusive rock is formed when magma cools in small pockets below Earth's surface. They cool very slowly, which allows large crystals to form. Some intrusive rocks have a spotted, speckled appearance because of these large crystals. Intrusive rocks have a rough texture and come in many colors.

This sculpture in Venice, Italy, was created from poryphry, an igneous rock that is both intrusive and extrusive. These rocks began to cool below Earth's surface but were forced to the surface by a volcanic eruption before they could finish hardening. This statue is at least a thousand years old.

Different Types of **IGNEOUS ROCKS**

People use intrusive rocks for many things, including construction. Granite is perhaps the most well-known intrusive igneous rock. It has been used for centuries as a building material. Granite can be many different colors, including gray, white, pink, or red. It is often spotted with crystals made from the minerals quartz, feldspar, and mica. Granite can be used in many different construction projects because it is hard and strong. The oldest known rock in the world is made of granite. It is nearly four billion years old!

This temple in Mahabalipuram, India, was built from granite in the seventh century.

Gabbro is another intrusive igneous rock that is used for building. It has large crystals and looks like granite, but gabbro is darker in color. Sometimes it looks blue or green. Gabbro has different minerals than granite. Important metals, such as nickel and platinum, are sometimes found in gabbro.

Rois-bheinn is the highest hill in Moidart, Scotland. It is composed of granite and gabbro.

Did You Know?

The Sierra Nevada mountain range in California was created from intrusive igneous rock.

Kimberlite is an unusual intrusive igneous rock. It forms in long pieces that look like pipes. It is dark in color and usually blue, green, or black. It forms deep beneath Earth's surface at 93 miles (150 kilometers) underground. At that depth, there is a lot of heat and pressure, which helps these rocks form. This intense heat and pressure often causes diamonds to form alongside kimberlite.

Kimberlite and diamonds often form together.

Why Are IGNEOUS ROCKS IMPORTANT?

Igneous rocks are not only important to the rock cycle but to people, as well. Humans have found many uses for them.

Culture and Civilization

Granite is one of the most widely used rocks on earth. People have been using it for thousands of years to build homes, churches, schools, and monuments.

Why Are IGNEOUS ROCKS IMPORTANT?

The walls of burial chambers inside the Pyramids of Giza in Egypt were constructed from granite.

Did You Know?

El Escorial Palace near Madrid, Spain, is the largest granite building in the world.

Native Americans and other ancient cultures used obsidian to make tools, masks, weapons, and jewelry. They even used it to make mirrors.

Basalt has been used for centuries to create sculptures on volcanic islands in the Pacific Ocean. The most famous of these are on Easter Island.

The statues on Easter Island are called moai, and they were built by the Rapa Nui people. The statues are actually full bodied even though only the heads are visible above ground.

28

Why Are **IGNEOUS ROCKS IMPORTANT?**

Scientific Knowledge

Scientists use igneous rocks to study Earth. These rocks can teach us much of what we need to know about volcanoes and their formation. They can also show us what is going on deep inside Earth.

The rock cycle has been shaping and reshaping Earth for millions of years. As magma continues to harden into igneous rocks, it ensures that the rock cycle will continue on for many years to come!

Devils Tower in Wyoming formed from intrusive igneous rock.

Glossary

asteroids—Small bodies made of rock and iron that travel around the Sun.

extrusive—A type of igneous rock formed when lava cools on the surface of Earth.

igneous rocks—Hot liquid underground minerals that have cooled and hardened into rocks.

intrusive—A type of igneous rock formed when magma cools and hardens under Earth's surface.

metamorphic rocks—Rocks that have been changed by heat and heavy weight.

meteorites—Rocks from outer space that reach Earth's surface.

minerals—Natural elements that are not animals, plants, or other living things.

plates—The moving pieces of Earth's crust and the top layer of Earth.

plutonic—Igneous rock formed when magma hardens under Earth's surface. Another name for intrusive.

sedimentary rocks—Layers of gravel, sand, silt, or mud that have been pressed together to form rocks.

Learn More

FURTHER READING

Dee, Willa. *Unearthing Igneous Rocks*. New York: PowerKids Press, 2014.

Nelson, Maria. *Igneous Rocks* (That Rocks!). New York: Gareth-Stevens Publishing, 2013.

Ostopowich, Melanie. *The Rock Cycle*. New York: Weigl Pub Inc., 2016.

Spilsbury, Richard. *Igneous Rocks* (Earth's Rocky Past). New York: PowerKids Press, 2015.

WEBSITES

ScienceViews.com: Types of Igneous Rocks
scienceviews.com/geology/igneous.html
Read more about the different types of igneous rocks and how they're formed.

Geology.com: Igneous Rocks
geology.com/rocks/igneous-rocks.shtml
See why igneous rocks look the way they do.

Science Kids: Igneous Rock Facts
sciencekids.co.nz/sciencefacts/earth/igneousrocks.html
Quick facts about igneous rocks.

Index

A

air, 5, 19, 20
asteroids, 15

B

basalt, 16, 21, 28

C

crust, 5, 8-10, 13, 16
crystals, 13, 17, 20, 22-24

E

Earth, 5, 8, 9, 10, 13, 15, 20, 22, 25, 29
earthquakes, 8
eruption, 5, 7, 10, 17, 19, 20, 21
extrusive rocks, 13, 17, 20

F

fault lines, 10

G

gabbro, 24
granite, 13, 23-24, 26-27

H

heat, 8, 10, 25

I

intrusive rocks, 13, 22-25

L

lava, 10, 16-17, 20
layers, 5, 9

M

magma, 5, 7-10, 13, 22, 29
mantle, 9, 10
Mars, 15
Mercury, 15
metamorphic rocks, 5, 8
meteorites, 15, 16
moon, 16

P

plates, 10
pressure, 8, 10, 25
pumice, 20

R

rock cycle, 7, 8, 26, 29

S

sedimentary rocks, 5, 8

V

Venus, 15
volcanoes, 7, 10, 17, 19, 29